This special hardcover edition limited to two hundred copies, of
which this is number ...154...

Emily Wilson

Balancing on Stones

By this author

Down Zion's Alley
Balancing on Stones

Colophon by Bruce Tucker

Balancing on Stones

Emily ⌊Wilson

The Jackpine Press
Timberlake Lane
Winston-Salem, North Carolina
1975

Acknowledgements
    Some of these poems have been published in *The Greensboro Review*, *Southern Poetry Review*, *The Pilot*, *Tar River Poets*, and *The Nickelodeon*.

Library of Congress Cataloging in Publication Data

Wilson, Emily, 1939-
    Balancing on stones.

    I. Title.
PS3573.I45693B3   811'.5'4   75-33651

Published by The Jackpine Press
Printed in Winston-Salem, N.C.,
by Clay Printing Company

CONTENTS

For my parents, Sarah and Clyde Herring,
and for my sister, Janis Herring Eberhardt

RESOLUTION

I am going to begin now
with the way light fails

to hold the sky, with the
brown dry leaves, still,

without speech. And watch
the day end in this faded out

far corner of my life,
when time gnaws at the bark

of carved branches. There
is so little to do:

I cannot dress the oak
again, stir up the heat

of the rich decay of leaves
and return each to a thin

connection with the trees.
I will not argue with the

energy of the creek currents.
Nor make conversation with

the criss-crossings of
bramble and bush.

The sky hangs over me
with a blank indifference

for the coming dark.
My bones are stiff, and

my words ache to be delivered.
If I could make my song heard

in the windless hollows,
I would praise man

and my arms would float from me
and touch the sky in calm victory.

A CHILD CRIES AT NIGHT

Old fire settles in the grate.
The dark smells earthen and cold.
Your little cries are under covers;
your nightmare flares into the night.

On Sligo Bay a buoy slides
over the world, belling the beast
who whines and blows; you hold your breath
to listen, locked into the rocking.

Past window and farm, riggings,
and cloudful hour, night rides you,
over and over.

IN SOME QUIET SPINNING PLACE

He will spend his final life
in the company of women; warm
October light will spill over

his work, lace his fingers
with the thin, silver web
of the spider; he will hear

talk at the level of a sigh;
and nothing loud would think
of walking by; he will sleep

or wake, or wake or sleep,
or wait for night to do
with him such hands of love

as he believes come true;
hope will stick like beggar's
lice to the inside of his need;

the sourwood will turn red,
and turn red; and he will
talk to himself, and think

of poems he should have said
for love, make them speak
in a language pressed

in vellum; in some quiet
spinning place he will find
morning dazzled with light,

and just when he has closed
her in a single room, morning
will turn him over, in her arms.

FOCUSING

At 500 ft. my 7x35 10 degree
wide field fully coated optics
got a line on that nuthatch
in her antics up and down
and around a wintering oak.
I braced myself and followed
her head-first down the trunk
until she reversed herself
and caught me at the bottom
when she was back up at the
top. By the time I got to where
she was, she was gone, and I
was dizzy enough not to interfere
with destination.

GROUNDED

Blue-jay, you are disruptive!
Your crest intrudes so jayishly
you'd think you owned the place.

What's a plain gray bird to do?
Ease off the feeder while you tell
the universe you're self-directed?

Throw your territorial rights
to the wind and come on down here
to ground level.

RICHMONDENA CARDINALIS

"Bright red male with black throat
is unmistakable." The birdbook
knows what the birds know.

This morning at the feeder
he showed himself in charge.
Her yellow-brown subdued
femaleness took a high perch
and waited. He busied himself.

Not even when a bunch of titmice
scattered seed and thrust up
their own dark crests did he
give way. All color revolved
around a red point.

Unless it was high on a winter
branch that a smaller red
distracted just enough to make
another presence known.

ELOISE ISHMAEL

She does not know
when she was born. She knows
Darlington County, South Carolina,
where her Daddy's people live.
They want to bring her home,
if home is where her mind is,
to the brown house and the dirt
yard, to the cousins rocking
on the porch.

Eloise Ishmael, age unknown,
knows the place
her slippers fit
under the bed,
and where she hides her money
in the old dark chest.

Her trust is absolute:
the right folks will take care
of her; she's taken care of them.
Sunday preaching's for sinners.
She'll not be one of them.
She's God's child and
he knows her.

Take me home she dreams
under the chinaberry tree
in the dirt yard
where she plays hopscotch
over and over.
I'm tired, you hear,
take me home.

HURTING

The dark child waits:
the mirror will change,
make beauty
for strangers to admire.
All the girls at school
want to be Queen.

The sun warms up
the last place
in the garden
where the slug leaves
his life
on the earth's last lonely run.

Bring back the morning
when the dolls came to tea.
Read to us the part
where the princess weeps
for joy.

Dress up in pink and organdy,
and we will go to a party.
The guests will all be
beautiful. Sunlight
will make circles in the air.

The deepest sound
is the silence
after the last cry.

LOVE POEM

If today you are
(lower than a snake's belly),
brother,
what's getting you down
(is this):

you are over-estimating
your potential!

Sit still and watch:
the sun comes up, shines;
the night settles, it's dark, and cold, too.
The blind man taps along with his cane,
glad to get to a corner he recognizes.
The widow takes her coffee alone.

Now what's eating you?
You think earth's
the wrong place
for hurting?

Brother, hitch up your belt
& walk on like
you've got some place to go
& are getting there.

ITEM

We've read about
the 84-year old black
woman who, after rais-
ing her brothers and
sisters and 60 years
as a maid, went back
to school and grad-
uated.

We may have read
the next year that she
died.

But we never read
how, alone, in her small
wood house, a rocker
drawn up to the light,
she studied her books.
And moved her mind from
the dirt yard and Mama's
chickens to the history
open in her lap, over a
clean white apron.

If we see her clear-
ing a space for her school
things, next to the water
glass, the eye shade, the
church calendar, if we see
her long past dark sitting
on the porch to say her
lessons, if we see her at
all,

we should call a poet
and tell
what we have not read.

FALLING

Wisteria falls, heavy and dark.
Old vines wrap around my heart.
I hide under the solemn branches
to crawl past memory and to hold
the trunk: here I begin, inside
the shade of Grandfather's last
morning. When his cane crosses
the porch and stops, my life stops.

Am I afraid to tell him I
found the place he wants to die?

I know just where the vine is tied,
loose it, and hold. I am free,
falling through layers of time,
my small tight body a message sent
across the silence.
I drop off, like a tear.
The sounds I do not make, he hears.
And satisfied, he turns away.

I have set my feet in a new place
a long road from the ears of death.
I make new bodies firm and fair
to swing in the wisteria
until I find again the branch
burning my hands, and feel the
passage of the fall. And know
to land with no one there to hear
how soundless and how far I come.

MYSELF, SMALLER THAN ANY SUN

The nut I found in my backyard
myself then a child
was miraculous:
a pale green stem sprouted

from the insides, mirroring
the great tree I wrapped around
my sleep for years and years,
on into this morning.

That something could grow
out of itself
without help from earth
was the first promise

in my life. Then I,
thin as any high branch,
began to take shape.
Putting down, going out.

I hold just in sight
this morning the sprouting
nut, feel the cool darkness
of its dreaming, and match

against it these old oaks
shading my grown-up's house.
On the first day of spring
the wind tore at the daffodils

and shook the red bud.
I stretched and stooped
on a long walk to see
the leafing, new green

tongues, eyes opening,
lips wet. Something tapped
out a message, singing.
My walk led me away from

the backyard of my childhood,
and I arrived at a lake,
overgrown with willow trees
and a wild tangle of brush.

In the brown water I saw
what I had never seen from
the field, a broad circle of
high tree tops, pointing

beyond themselves. At water's
edge I looked for signs of
life among the weeds, and saw
myself, smaller than any sun.

OFF ROSSES POINT

A boy fell or jumped
from this high bank,
where cattle feed
right to the edge.
He is gone, and will
not come home tonight,
not singing from Flaherty's
after the last round's
drunk and the last stranger
turns to his own.
Fear does not stand
on the edge
or ride the far crest
but hides in the throat
of a song
a boy sings
while he walks home.

FOR BARBARA

1932 - 1975

Trees shimmer green
and the birds fuss;
May holds the moment
in her teeth, gives it
a shake, and buds fall
out, open; morning
wakes cool and wet.

There you are walking
in the yard, here you care
for a child, just in
the shadows, you speak
to a friend.

We shall live out
your life and hold you
in memory dearer than
the honeysuckle air.
Your motions give
shape to our days,
your wisdom sticks
to the inside of
our need.
You are as real
as this May morning.
Barbara, be with us.

LOCKING UP

I know when the first chill
blows off the pines, it's time
to come inside.

Shut every door, draw the curtains
in the backroom, turn the key,
stir up the fire.

The children hold one another;
their long flowered gowns dance
and hide.

Light is closed in a single room;
dreams are plumped and stuffed
in an old chair.

I do not know what the big dog
waits for in the cold silence
or when the horses shy

at the white moth's flutter.
I do not know.

THE JULIE POEMS

So many times
she's come to me
when I sat hoping
for the Muse.

I go about the house
in dreams
learned
before her birth:

her small warm hands
touch my legs,
and she's there,
steady and loyal.

In a room
full of strangers,
I bend down and
we talk,

pull in around us
a cocoon of secrets.
When something
rattles me

and I stumble around
trying to adjust
to the dark,
I find her

making a place
for me
in her own bed.
After she sleeps,

I wait for a long time
until the Julie poems
write themselves.

HOME

The blue letter box hides
the years her boy was sent away.
Color pictures from far off
carry his message: I want to come home.
On cold afternoons she locks herself
in her room and lines up the pictures
on her bed. He's sure to come today.

FROM A FAR PLACE

for Maya Angelou

So many mornings ago
I was the little girl
on the Avenue, sweeping
the sidewalk.

You balanced a basket
on your head
like an Egyptian woman
in my school book.
Your thin dark skirt
rode between your legs.

The sweat you wiped away
clean with a white handkerchief
rolled in your sleeve.

We looked
back and forth.
I think
we never spoke.

Now you have come
from a far place
to visit home:
your dress dazzles,
your rings like diamonds,
are diamonds.
We drink white wine,
as in a movie.
You speak
a beautiful and strange
way.

I watch
your body leave,
taller than anyone's,
your turban in the sun.

I in my child's body
run after you,
balance in your shadow
like a shadow.

PSYCHIATRIC COUNSELING

I'd like to
pop a persimmon
gulp a grape
and rout out the chipmunks
chipping away at winter.
If it'd make you happy
I'd skin a squirrel
chop some kindling
and dangle upside down
from the oak
outside your window.

Help's on the way.
I can tell
by the rings
on the woollybears.
Be still, keep your eyes
open, listen:
here comes hope
walking a rail fence;
laughter's rolling around
in a hollow log;
energy's holed up,
secure.

LOVE

While the tennis match drones on
in the wet heat of North Carolina,
two flies make love inside the
secrets of a Coca Cola can.

Pause that refreshes!
Let the sun shine, the sweat pop,
let the players grunt and fall,
the spectators turn their heads,

but life goes on in vintage syrup,
someone's leftovers too good
to miss, and the flies swoon,
rubbing their legs in ecstasy.

Our happy hour! Drink up
and come inside my 12 oz. can
with me, and let's make love.
The score is oh and oh.

VISITING POET

I am all morning
in the kitchen
for one who hungers
for black beans
and white sunlight.

These visiting poets
strain
the local imagination.
I have boiled up
my nerve
and set it out to cool.

Twice this morning
I have burned my thumb
on a metaphor
and rhymed the dough.

Turn down the heat.

BALANCING ON STONES

Perhaps the light bending
   in the wheat
or the pale undersides of
   summer leaves
filled up the old silences
   between us.
We found our way easy,
   across small streams,
walking in field daisies,
   naming birds.

Then we came to the place
   no human talk
makes sound without pushing
   beyond the limits
to where pain lies, dark
   as the creek banks,
pushing from a darker source,
   washing upon us,
adrift, frightened, quick,
   balancing on stones.

ANNIVERSARY PRESENT

These Beautiful Nepalese Bronze
Foo-Dogs might be just right,
or a pair of boudoir bottles,
imported spoons, sculptured
strawberries (Strawberries in
the Snow), a mink coat, tapestry.
The Horchow Collection comes
to me in prices no one can do
without: $500 for a rocking horse!
I'd buy a baby just to have that
one! I'll close my eyes and flip
a million dollars. Wife, you'll
have your heart's desire. That's
my desire.

THE DIFFERENCE

Is it better for old leaves
to die, drop off, and decay
in darkening earth, or like
the oak leaf, wither brown,
crinkled, but holding on
when the gray winter sky
yawns over the grave and
the earth steeps and lays
for spring?

BLACKWOMAN

Blackbone, barebone,
shining. Hard and
quick as the blade.

Work, work in the
pale fields, in the pine
logs, oozing, work boiled

on the back fire.
Woman black as the wild
hogs rooting under dreams.

Woman moves from field
to bed from dream to
death, to joy. Light

as the song of the
guinea hens, sorrowing,
sorrowing. Woman black

as the open door when
life runs out at night,
no one calls back,

no one knows who leaves,
who enters. Moves in
shadows and dew-web

to plant, to pick,
to carry, like wind in
thistles. Windwrapped

round the pinesong.
Straight-stalk, shining
in water, shining in

daylight and moonlight.
Blackbone, barebone.
Woman, the sun bursts black.

SILENCE

Silence floats on the water: underneath
the Atlantic rolls, muffled and large.
The last sound has been emptied out;
   the cargo ship breathes in the sun,
   rust works in her chains.

The islands hump their backs in old
sleep. Inishmore rises on one arm,
watches. Hours turn over, time unwinds,
   falls loose. Morning
   bursts out of bounds.

Across Kilronan space divides inside
itself. Ragged ground coughs up rocks,
broken and heavy. Lichens change,
   claw and hold on. A thin
   blue skin rounds the land.

Houses wake, thrust chimneys north,
send up heat, musty and gray. One
road is drawn, a single silver thread,
   passing through the sun's eye.
   Earth pushes against seams.

Dough rises on the table, water
boils, the udder of the cow hangs
full. Black currachs ride low
   under the waves, weighted
   with the shining catch.

Inishmore steeps, settles, darkens
in the sun. Light stretches from
cove to cove, thins at the top.
   Two miles inland, rock walls
   fall down with the tides.

An old woman opens a window and
   watches for a long time.

FOR BEING A WOMAN

For being a woman she was not hanged
but left to observe her toiletries

in the narrow cell of Kilmainham Jail.
She dared to drive her horses in the street

and lead a Revolution: the fetching Creamery
Maid of Sligo and the beauty of Yeats' wild eye.

Contradictions understood by the old peasant woman
placing two eggs on the coffin of Countess Markievicz:

"I said when the little black hen would lay
I'd bring the eggs to Madame at the hospital.

Now she's dead but I want her to have them."

Ireland yokes to beauty simplest good.

POOLSIDE

Taking a breath and
putting your face
in water requires
more courage than
God has any right
to expect.
But God's substitute
is on fire this summer
to teach the five-year-olds
to swim.

His lean body
oils its way around the pool;
he rubs his legs, and smiles.
His white teeth flash,
and every mother watches.

Meanwhile, the child,
God's orphan,
shivers, prepared to do
all that is asked of him today.
The golden sun tan king
is ready; behold
he walks on water.

HELP

The phone rings,
the doorbell rings,
the world rings.
Everybody is calling
this morning.
Wanting to speak
to the lady of the house:

Is she at home?
When do you expect her?

Not today.
She's chopping wood
and not to be disturbed.
She's out back
chopping wood.

WANTED:

Unacknowledged legislator
of the world; maker of dreams;
prince des nuées; inebriate of
air; mature person. Settled but
open to inquiry. Modest but am-
bitious. Must show evidence of
sullen craft. Salary negotiable.
Apply Drawer E, New Haven, Conn.

BEGINNING AN EPIC

for Archie

The place had not been defined
for him when he came to teach.

Hot, an August afternoon, lost
on the nameless roads, looking

for home. That he would come to
sleep and wake here, for a time,

seemed only something he dreamed,
far away, in some other body.

Now the fruits of his dreaming
grow in the green fields, and

his care is known even by the
insects. The idols that small

men made grew dusty and fell
down; and he stayed in the

shadows until time to sit down,
to listen, then to speak.

His quiet voice sounds the
intensity of our need, and will

echo in rooms and out in the
open when he is gone. Like

warriors who travel long and
far in search of the great

task, may he travel back to
this place, defined by his absence.

THE DOCTOR'S STORY

Children don't believe in me.
I tell the truth.
I tell them it hurts.
They believe their mother's promise:
they will wake up in a playhouse,
too small for doctors.

My hands, my clean instruments
will make them well.
Please understand.
I have a little girl, a boy,
who love me.
I am good to them,
I read stories, we play.
And when they are sick,
they come to me.

Now I must go back
under the lights.
The child sleeps,
in a dream.
When he wakes up
my scar will be on him.
And all that will matter to him
will be the scar.

TO A FRIEND

I don't walk past your house
anymore. I am tired of wanting
to see you. Your light plays
tricks on me, it is not you.

Your laughter stopped at the top.
I held my breath for you
to say, go on, go on.
I can't go on.

Voices distract me.
The children want to play.
They told me you would get well;
we crossed our fingers.

Children can't bridge
this distance between us;
when you died
you were old.

I have come to tea.
My cup is filled with a shadow,
a thin, blank moon.
Dry flowers begin to bloom.

Turn out the light.

BELIEVE IT OR NOT

In South Carolina
a boy rides down the Interstate,
riding the back of a motorcycle,
a small gray monkey hanging on.

Under a shadowless noon sky
they are having lunch.
passing a Pepsi back and forth,
leaning to the wind.

And miles down the highway
the motor hums:

the monkey pressed to the boy's chest,
the boy weeping;
the boy moving his lips,
the monkey listening.

RABBITS

A rabbit
gets on fine
with his family,
fathers them,
provides for them,
and doesn't have
to be coaxed out
at night for a run
(leaving no traces
in the tall grasses):
then if I seem
to twitch my nose
& jump at the sound
of your heavy feet,
don't think I'm
permanently shutting
myself off
from the world. I'll
come out when
you're gone.

THE BREAD AND BUTTER OF LIFE

Phyllis makes magic:
add, stir, knead, and
under a light cloth
life rises, waits.
She brings perfection
to the table, without
fanfare, lets it speak
for itself.
If God were hungry,
he'd have Phyllis for his wife!
She has the touch
no man
can do without.
Her bread's
the envy
of the neighborhood
and rises
in the dreams
of other women.

LUNCHEON

The girls were having sherry
and exchanging
talk of
their most recent husbands
when one of them
started crying
and had to be taken home.

SATURDAY

Rain since before breakfast,
the children carrying
their complaints from
room to room,

the woman standing
at the sink looking out,
the man deciding what
to do: a friendly scene

if life is friendly;
but the rain does not
care that the family wants
it to go away

and darkens the tree trunks
hour by hour.
A cloud of red bud
floats on the hillside,

the fire going out;
daffodils cannot hold
up their heads. In the
yard a child's toy

rusts and reminds the
mother standing at the
window of a birthday,
something gone.

In a little while
the creek will push out
of its banks and flood
the low bushes where

quail come up each
morning. The sound
the rain makes
is not like any voice

heard in the house,
but nevertheless
drills on,
fixing the day.

PLAY IT BY EAR

If you're not much for thesis and antithesis
(statement leaves you out in the cold),
play it by ear:

shades of meaning along the edges,
skin prickles in hot water, flashes
into childhood (the big yard, the woods violets),
familiarity at crossroads, shivers of recognition.
When someone walks across your grave, brother,
you are the first to know.

If you don't read music, stand next to someone
who does, taking you up and down the scale until
you feel the differences: bells, bellows, star, stare,
cell, shell, glow, glare, shine, china, fall, fell.
When the flag goes up and nobody else can remember
the words, the drum will beat in your head.

The insect with his antennae out recoils
in a hurry, rolls up into a dull brown ball.
The chipmunk lies dead until the cat gives up,
then puffs out his sides and escapes with his joke.
Sure there's a lesson here for you: be quiet and listen.

If you pass by a bird and arch your neck
you're connecting. When a nut drops on the roof,
jump. Subjects and verbs have a natural order
completed by direct or indirect objects:
anything less leaves your nerves out of joint.

Do you think you're getting it? Hang loose.
Put your ear to the railroad track.
Something's comin'.

AFTER TEA

for Germaine Brée

When you left, the jays
started quarreling.
Such blue racket
distracted us for a while,
and then we turned

to wash the cups
and tidy up the crumbs.
The little girls danced
like figures
on a music box,

dark heads, dark eyes.
I wondered
if they still heard
those lovely French songs.
Until I saw in the shadows

the movement of your hands,
gestures
hanging in air.
Directing the morning's
harmony.

MOTHER LOCKS THE DOOR

We are safe.
Mother locks the door
and banks the fire.
We shiver under mounds,
slide our feet deep
into cold corners,
muffle our prayers.
Deliver us from evil.
From the ghosts hiding
under the creek bank
and the howl in the field.
The fire jumps, lights up
our faces. We whisper,
don't be afraid.
Outside it's black dark.
When we sleep,
the cinders glow,
and something scratches
at the window.

FROM NOW ON

I'm going to concentrate
on things that work:
boiling water takes out
blueberry stain and hilling
up tomato plants makes them
stronger. Blue-eyed grass
blooms in nameless weeds, and
sassafras grows in three kinds
of leaves. There is nothing
under the sun which feels like
new school books and a lead
pencil. And if that is not
enough, try hands, the Monarch
butterfly, and candlelight.
From now on there's no use
worrying about anything else.

DOLLY McPHERSON

It is a long way to the River,
a long way to Louisiana and
to your one-hundred year old
farmland; past the rotted fence
posts, past the shining river basin,
the old sun in a red and dying field.

And going back is the song I learned
in childhood, on the porches down
Zion's Alley. Dolly, I heard your
voice, but we were lost to each other,
though I sat as close to your black
sisters as a sister; and the space

across was lonely and deep.

UP-ONE

If I ride my bike with no hands,
someone can always ride standing
on the seat. If I walk a fence,
someone can always walk it back-
wards. Balance a broom on my
middle finger, and someone else
can balance it on his nose.
Today I'm going to climb a tree
and twist the tail of the first
squirrel who gets in my way!

PLAY

The child is the mother now,
grown up, tall, the strong one.
The mother is the child,
slipped down into her robe.

They play on the floor
like a mother and child.
The child (really the mother)
dresses her doll,
cannot tie the ribbon,
needs help from the mother
(really the child).

All afternoon, on the floor,
in the fading light,
they play,
until it's time for supper.
The doll is put away,
and the child cries.

BUCKLE MY SHOE

Julie is at her numbers:

How many legs on a squirrel?
How many teeth in a baby?

How many stars blinked last night?
How many ghosts on the moon?

How many birthdays will happen to me?
How many cousins know my name?

How many petals hold a flower?
How many rainbows make July?

How many nights will I sleep?
How many dreams before I die?

Mama, count for me.
Count for me, Mama.

SEPTEMBER MORNING

Webbed eaves, corners,
and branches, fields,
laced together.
The stitching

goes on past sundown;
morning composes
silver wheels in space.
Circles, arcs, tangles,

lifelines
out and back.
In old timbered shadows
or high over dark water

rhythms connect, carry.

Arachne
despaired of perfection,
and hanged herself;
she spins

a maiden's life forever.

To come on an abandoned line
is to know
the next motion:
seeding air.

The juices of morning
are hardening,
jeweled.

CHOICES

Anything lovely will do:
the leaf spinning midway
between ground and tree;
the cold blue November;
thin branches like the
arms of dancers; the cat's
yawn. For the day's energy,
the impulse to move along.

Eloise, for example, feeling
low, pulls up close to the
fire, and she's home, folding
her black cracked hands warm
in her lap. Or think of the
widow, rising to an empty house,
dressing immaculately, for the
example she sets for her daughters
in their time. I know a young man,
angry, bitter, but his laughter's
free, like a boy's.

In an average week pain's everywhere:
the child wakes up from a nightmare;
Uncle John Henry sleeps strapped in
the chair, his heart gone; what you
read in the paper, what you fear.

So you count on coming home to a
good supper, a good wife; to read to
the children; to watch the fire.
Not to be startled or made to go out.
Anything lovely will do.

TEMPLE-BUILDING

I make for you
a new shape
of words
placed in exact
order, hoping
to join
earth and sky.

My long reaching
extends from this
morning to an
earlier time without
you and to a later
time when you are gone.
I touch

each word, feel its
motions, and bring it
in its flame
to you to keep burning
for me. May this small
but certain shape
light up

the sky, rooted in dark
earth, until cloud and
root move. And wherever
you are, I am, will be
the place of the burning
temple, giving off steady
warmth and light,

to see by, to live by.

Emily Herring Wilson, a native of Columbus, Georgia, lives in Winston-Salem, North Carolina. A graduate of the University of North Carolina at Greensboro and Wake Forest University, she has taught at Wake Forest and Salem College. She has been a participant in the state's *Poetry in the Schools Program* and a reader for the North Carolina Arts Council. Her first book of poetry, *Down Zion's Alley,* was published in 1972; her work has been included in *New Southern Poets,* edited by Guy Owen and Mary Williams. She teaches a course in Recent American Poetry at Reynolda House in Winston-Salem. She is married to Edwin G. Wilson and is the mother of three children, Eddie, Sally, and Julie. She is frequently at home.